Also by George Spain:

Dreaming the Fire Away

A man is never real when
dreaming the fire away
sitting quietly
as dark rings round
his silence strains to see
something beyond the light

George Spain

Ideas into Books: Westview®
Kingston Springs, Tennessee

Ideas into Books®
W E S T V I E W
P.O. Box 605
Kingston Springs, TN 37082
www.publishedbywestview.com

ISBN 978-1-62880-126-2

First edition, August 2017

Printed in the United States of America on acid free paper.

to

Jackie

Acknowledgments

Most especially I thank Mary Catharine Nelson, my stalwart publisher who has woven her skills through all my works. Also thanks go to Louise Colln, a fine writer and friend, and to the Williamson County Critique Group, the Carnegie Writers Group, and to my friends at the Green Hills Library.

Contents

Foreword

Leningrad 1941-42 was my first published poem. It appeared in *Soviet Life* in 1969. I tried to get Jackie, my wife, to defect with me since I didn't seem to be appreciated in the U.S. She refused. Then in 1981, *Cumberland Poetry Review* published *Crow Hunting*. With that I felt appreciated and gave up thoughts of defecting.

In the seventies I began writing short stories, later a novel, then children's books and satires. But poetry has continued to draw me back to its freedoms for truths and beliefs not always easily expressed in other forms.

For better or worse here are the ones I've chosen for *Dreaming the Fire Away*. A few were written just for fun but most are about loving, living, dying, God and the Devil.

Hope you enjoy them, some will make you smile, some may make you scowl but please, if you don't like it don't tell me and don't drop it in a garbage can; please pass it on to a homeless person standing on the corner selling whatever he is selling.

Dreaming the Fire Away

A man is never real when
Dreaming the fire away
Sitting quietly
As dark rings round
His silence strains to see
Something beyond the light.

Then twisting the dark
Rings tighter round the light
Darkness comes
To sit quietly
And dream of men
Dreaming the fire away.

Creation

Once
For the lark of it
The Great Black-Thighed Sky
Did its own thing
Which is really how it all began
For the rest of us.
For sometime now
Naked
It had been lying around
Spread eagle
Bored stiff
And getting old
Waiting for something
To come along
To make it giggle forever
And feel young again.
Hell
You can just wait so long
For your boat to come in
For the First Coming
For the Resurrection
For the Second Coming
For the Meaning of Existence.
So for fun it spun itself
Around into a pretzel
Touching places
It never knew existed
When all of a sudden
All hell broke loose
And heaven too
And so did earth
And that's how it all began.

Ah! Summer Begins, Begins!

And all is as it was before winter's wearing away
The sow bellied suns
Heigh-ho-hurrah, thrusting, swelling, kicking,
Meaning of it all,
The mercy in it all,
Adoring the mercy in us all
Crambling up the cradle's side shouting,
"It's lust that makes a man,
And lust is where he ends."
As all the black-blooded earth throbs, spreads and opens.
And the Sweat of Summer's
Sour, smelly, pitthighbrow
Plows deep into the blood-sweet earth;
Dripping, flooding beneath the moving grass
Swarming with wild-brown bees dancing tall tales
As they buzz their busy business with wild-brown boys
Who dare their devils above in trees and beneath the water falls
While the sun dries all their glory away,
And clouds climb and climb and collide into tomorrow
Then slide back again into today:
Wavering weaving in images walking on water;
While all the while the trod and throb of summer lifts
Old men and lambs upward into the sky
And there for a little bit
They stride upon their pride
Which never stops.

Kings X and Time out

Kings X and time out
Where are the back slapping lads
Who rolled me down the bumpbacked hills
When I was King on the mountain
With always a shout in my heart?

Where are those blind-man bluff days
When Jacks were nimble and quick
And never a dragon was feared
As I straddled my fathers shoulders
With never a rhyme in my mind

That our London Bridged Summers were falling
And all our Happy Humpty Dumptys
Were breaking never again to rise
And all the saints who patty-caked were growing
With forever a remembering in my heart.

Then Ends and Begins Again

On that side of summer's beginning
When children laugh while playing
Their fabulous ways toward death
And griefs are fixed to tears
Though never wiped away
Heaven hangs on a high hill
Where winds whirl faith away
Before the last cock crow
And time runs down into a hollow
Of the heart until it is filled
                              then ends.
Within the heat of winter's spinning
Golden nets are set for flying unicorns
On whose horns a shibboleth
Of fire forked light appears
In words that melt away
All jacks of frost until
The tears of spring lose their way
From out the eye and flow
Into a flood where flowers grow
And time which is never stilled
                              begins again.

Walking in the Woods

Walking in the woods
On a fall evening
The trees and earth and air
Are orange and yellow and red
We laugh at the same moment
We say, "I love you!"

Listening to Whippoorwills

Listen to the whippoorwills calling beyond the windows
As they did last night and the night before in the woods
Around the house where the great horned owl is hooting.
I touched you but you rolled away, your back to me,
Your heart broken in pieces, like white porcelain.
I had promised you to be true forever,
My mother's ring is there to prove it:
The one you took from your finger yesterday
And placed on the dressing table, where it glimmers,
As a silver thorn in the moonlight.
That day when I told you, all that was in your eyes
Has disappeared and not returned.
I had promised you five children and I did not fail you,
But they can never repair what has been broken.
Yes, the whippoorwills are calling to one another
In the darkness in the tall trees high above the house,
And the owl is calling and calling and there is no answer.

Seven Small Stones Smooth as Skin

There,

No,

There,

Right in front of you.

Look quickly or you'll miss them.

Seven small stones smooth as skin

Skipping swiftly across that still pond.

Do you see them?

Soon they'll slow and sink below the surface.

Damn!

Soon as I said soon they sank

That's strange

Do you see

Seven small Stones scarcely stir the surface.

Heart Bleed and Blood Red

Heart bleed and blood red in my red heart

Bleeding beauty white in the night sunk bed

Where hangs tight the twitching tongue lick

And rut lock on golden mouths making

Love live and last as we bear heaven's children

Upward and die on our cries in the night

Before death turns white our red bones

Lying naked as water waiting under the arc

Of your coming for fish turned men to turn

From me above our sinking bed where soon

We bleed our love away together

And rise the next morning to heaven.

St. John's Churchyard

We started out together and will end that way

Coupling in grass in air

And sun and rain will not wear

Away our boxwood bed in St. John's Churchyard

Will not turn white our bones grown

Red with wine and love the birds

Will still be there in trees

And air and singing the old gray stones

Their names and dates will still be there

The cedars and magnolias

The falling cherry blossoms like moonlight

In air will still be there the old

Old bells will ring

And ring forever our day

Will still be there and we will end that way

Three Old Men on the Elk's Club Porch

Three old men on the Elk's Club porch,
Rock on a summer's day.
The sun is hot but cannot scorch,
Their daily rock away.

They rock forever and anon,
Through days of long ago,
An ancient rocking marathon,
Their tales rock to and fro.

Joe Bob decries the youth today,
"What are they coming to?
Its drugs and no respect I say,
We need to hang a few!

"Its more hell and fire and brimstone,
The preachers need to preach,
And leave that socialism alone,
Which all the young ones teach.

"Remember that old Campbellite?
He made you feel the heat.
Hell, I once wet my bed in fright,
And had to hide the sheet."

Just then, a funeral goes by.
Their rockers cease to rock,
In honor of old friends who die.
Twelve - strikes the courthouse clock!

"Well Squire, they're burying Miss Erma,"
Old Sam says kinda slow.
And Squire, who likes English humor,
Winks, "Yes, she's dead y'know."

Oh My Spirit

Oh my spirit
See through my eyes
Your wild hair wilding
Above my face
And hear our quick breaths
Mixing in the air
Round us
And our cries
Of lust and life.

The Devil Is a Gentleman

The Devil is a gentleman on a fine blood horse,
He sits on an English saddle of course.
His coat is blood red, His weskit pure white,
His boots are knee high, His spurs shining bright.

Handsome He is with His coal black hair,
And close cut beard and smile so fair,
He doffs His top hat to all who He sees,
To rich and to poor for He believes,

One should not look wicked, One, should look kind,
For His face tires easily looking wicked all of the time.
In the old days His face was so scary it made babies cry,
But now people smile up at Him, as He smiles from on high.

He knows He must change to keep up with Man
Who's changing faster than even God can
Or so Man believes, he believes he knows all,
That God and the Devil are both falderal.

Now that he's lost faith in the hot fires of Hell,
Man just wants to text and to tweet and to send emails,
And talk on cell phones and spend more than he's got,
So now the Devil's a Banker, who lends money from a pot.

He leaves Hell every morning with gold coins in His purse,
And rides forth with a smile to see whom He can coerce,
With their souls as their collateral for all that He loans,
Which, one day He'll collect on and He'll smile at their groans.

For the Devil's a gentleman on a fine blood horse;
He sits on an English saddle of course.
His smile draws Man to Him; His smile is so fair,
Handsome He is with His coal black hair.

The Mask That Hides the Face

The mask that hides the face
Stares back without a trace of love
As though it would disgrace
The mask to let the face show love
While underneath the mask
Tears from the face do beg for love.

Lord Lord

Lord Lord
It's a beautiful river   but wild
No man's laid a hand on it

Lord it's full of surprises
The flow is unpredictable   swift to slow
Then swift again   without warning

Lord don't you love its sudden bends
No man charted this river
No god   no fate   no mother earth
It twists in the earth like lightning
Maybe that's what made it   lightning

Lord I love how at times it curves softly
You can never see too far ahead
You keep looking for something new   or beautiful

And Lord we've found it
So let's stop and rest awhile
Let's strip down
Let's lie naked under the water
Let's feel the current flow over and around us

Lord knowing you   you'll want to dance

Lord you might even tell me you love me

Lord Lord

Now Strike the Midnight from My Eye

Now strike the midnight from my eye

Tongue speak truth rather than lie

Body be proud that you are man

War with God as long as you can.

Black Boar

Deep in darkness   deeper than shadows

    quiet

        listening

Hearing dreams curve   relax

Then catch tight at last

On tusks   curving   always curving

    inward

        tighter

Rooting time away   his small eyes burn

Remembering with fire

Almost the laurel thicket has light forever

    a burning bush

        almost

But only blackness and dumbness

Grunting   slowly   grunting

Something that has no meaning

    over

        and over

Wallowing deeper into the cool mountain

Of his birth   floating on dreams

His ancient reflection flowing away in darkness

   quiet

     listening

Hearing horns blowing away the forest

   black

     bristling.

Winter Wren

Through streaks
Of light and shadow
Above the laurel thicket
A quick fleck of brown flits
From limb to limb
Her weight a puff of feathers
Comes to perch near her nest
One green limb bends
Letting light flow down
Onto two yellow tusks
Wet with blood
It is then the wren
Raises her tiny head to sing
A rapid tinkling warble
A high quick succession of trills
A tremble sound long sustained
That warns then ends
And from far down the mountain
Through forest and mist
Comes a murmur of running hounds.

The Spirit

From 1817 to 1828, the John Bell family of Adams Station, Tennessee, was haunted by a spirit that eventually became known as the Bell Witch. There were nine Bell children. Among them, eleven year-old Betsy, was the one most tormented by the spirit. On a Sunday night, after a day of preaching, Reverend James Gunn, was invited to have supper with the Bells. When they finished eating, Reverend Gunn began to read scriptures; as he did the spirit spoke to Betsy who was standing beside an open window – watching, listening, and thinking.

Minister

Deuteronomy, chapter eighteen, verses ten through fourteen: There shall not be found among you anyone that maketh his son or his daughter pass through the fire, or that useth divination, or an observer of times, or an enchanter, or a witch, or a charmer, or consulter with familiar spirits, or a wizard, or a necromancer. For all that do these things are an abomination unto the Lord: and because of these abominations the Lord thy God doth drive them out from before thee. Thou shalt be perfect with the Lord thy God. First Samuel, twenty- eight, verses seven through twenty five: Then said Saul unto his servants, Seek me a woman that hath a familiar spirit...

Spirit

O dear sweet, sweet girl, hear if you have ears to hear Old Sugarmouth's dark words rambling on and on in the night, seeking to strip sins away with King James, driving Deuteronomy in and out of wood, plaster, air, and flesh.

Betsy

Delicate and transparent as fine white skin, are lace curtains finely woven. Delicate finely spun webs covering windows black with night. Delectably, deliciously delicate, to touch, to taste, to wrap round face, arms, legs, to watch through, to rest a spider; delicate and soft, as white, soft hands immersed in whiteness. Watching others gathered together to discharge their curse. Minister, father, mother, brothers, sisters playing their child's game, searching for that to stay that which pulls them together in blood, in secret in word of God.

Minister

And the woman said unto Saul, I saw gods ascending out of the earth...

Spirit

Heed my words one by one, if a god comes on the earth your young bush will be burned with fire. For often he will make you pass through the fire in innocence, binding your long legs with wild grape vines, his face above you sweating and grunting. O sweet girl he who is continually coming up and out upon the earth shall be brought low before I go.

Betsy

Delectably watching him: tall, shrewd in his straight strength of body and mind. He listening intently without hearing the ineradicable rhythm of God's word, hearing beyond the tall windows open onto summer's hot darkness, beyond night winds whisperings, rumpling lace and skin, beyond the peeps of beasts and men.

Minister

Then Saul fell straightway all along on the earth, and was sore afraid, because of the words of Samuel: and there was no strength in him for he had eaten no bread all the day, nor all the night. And the woman came unto Saul, and saw that he was sore troubled, and said unto him, Behold, thine handmaid hath obeyed thy voice, and I put my life in my hand and have harkened unto thy words which thou spakest unto me...

Betsy

Riding above the winds and sounds of night he sits: strong arms folded, left hand hidden, right hand white in the light of the lamp, resting gently upon his sleeve, gently upon an arm heavy with strength and pleasure. Neither fearing, nor hating, nor loving, listening only to the amazement of a remembering, reviving in whispers over and over.

Spirit

Blood of my blood, bone of my bone, flesh of my flesh, know you not you are the temple of God, if any man defiles the temple of God him shall God destroy.

Minister

Leviticus, twenty-six through twenty-seven: And the soul that turneth after such as have familiar spirits, and after wizards, to go a whoring after them, I will even set my face against that soul, and will cut him off from among his people. Sanctify yourselves therefore, and be ye holy: for I am the Lord your God...

Betsy

In their circle they sit as for protection. Bound not by hands, nor by the minister's paralytic droning, nor by the six sides of simple, though skillfully woven, weatherboard that vertically and horizontally fixes their circle as a cross into the rich, red land; nor even by their common source of earth and blood, but by the known and unknown knowledge of their secrets. Larger than shadows he sits. Listening. A conqueror conquered in his own strength; he who conquered forest and land and family. Sitting. His face turned half away.

Minister

And if a man lie with a beast, he shall surely be put to death: and ye shall slay the beast. And if a woman approach unto any beast, and lie down thereto, thou shall kill the woman, and the beast: they shall surely be put to death; their blood shall be upon them...

Spirit

You that have ears to hear, let them hear: the desolation of houses where the beasts of the forests lie and owls dwell and satyrs dance; hear the wild beasts of the air cry in their desolation and dragons in their pleasant palaces. Your time is near at hand. Your days shall not be prolonged.

Betsy

Shades of red and black and white flicker and fade. The lace draws tighter round. Dead still they sit. Watching. Mouths open. Wondering at the milk and honey under their tongues.

Spirit

O dear sweet girl: hear rather the genesis and revelations that come flickering from my mouth; a serpent's tongue testing the dark for the hidden one who comes from the forest running, leaping, shedding his skin of sin, drunk in his tremendous whiteness; a new child of God freshly risen from the Red River, running, leaping like a rutting deer. My testing tongue tells he comes grunting in glory. He comes and goes in the dark. His shadow swirls and turns black.

Betsy

Will he not turn and see through the lace, a face faced by enemies smiling on suffering and winking their eyes, that hate? Yes! They open their mouths wide and say, our eyes have seen through the delicate and transparent lace and forest. Nothing has been hidden from those who watch in secret the bright red spot of light rising in darkness. Will he set his face forever away? Turn now and see through the tears and sweat that leave their drippings on cheek and breast. Sorrows and shouts have been heard and not forgotten. Let them not smile. Let them rather shout in joy for the joy given!

Spirit

The sounds of our beloved! He comes leaping over mountains, dancing upon hills. Flowers appear before him, singing birds are all around, the turtle's voice is heard in the land and our vines have tender grapes. He is a buck feeding upon lilies and I am the Lily of the Valley. The earth trembles and shakes.

Betsy

The breeze stops. The single, coal-oil lamp, clean and bright, mingles its scents with others secretly hanging in the still and heavy air and gives life to shadows joining together without definition or darkness.

Spirit

Behold! The hidden one comes leaping and dancing hand in hand with all things created in the beginning. He comes. He comes. leaping and dancing upon the earth. The earth heaves and opens. Behold! He comes! He comes!

Betsy

Bound round and round with lace - squealing and panting for joy!

Minister

A man also or a woman that hath a familiar spirit, or that is a wizard, shall surely be put to death: they shall stone them with stones: their blood shall be upon them...

Betsy

To and fro, to and fro, to and fro, rocking in rhythm to the word of the Lord.

Spirit

O sweet, sweet love, dip now your hand into the Red River. Know you the hidden one comes for burial in water, love and blood. Know you his sacrifice, is your salvation. Know you God's will. Rise and sacrifice an offering unto God, young, white, delicate as lace.

Betsy

Listening now to his eternal listening. With him, as one, listening to whisperings rending round all in all. Listening to lace and skin tearing away layer by layer. Listening until at last all is stripped bare and the hidden one rises fresh and white – Listen! - Aha now they all listen and watch. And now all their mouths are open. Behold! Behold! Behold! He turns! He rises! He comes looking full upon a sweet, sweet, white face clean of lace.

Spirit

Hear now you that have ears to hear! Hear now the leaping and the dancing! Hear now the genesis and the exodus! Hear now, the hidden one, coming and going in the dark!

Minister

Exodus twenty-two, verse eighteen: Thou shalt not suffer a witch to live.

A Miracle

Alone in myself
I pray
For a miracle.
Children
And heaven and earth
Have no eternity.
Born in decay
I am
My final offering.
Black over red
Consumes
The day.
Now toward evening
The miracle
Is my prayer.

Our Fleeing Freedom

Our fleeing freedom is first set free
By the hump-back horseman
Of heaven and hell
Who breaks loose the soft sacks
Hooked tight in our mothers
And makes us cry the lusty cry of life
As our mothers watch in unbelief
And our fathers wonder at their fathers
As we creep up the cradle sides
To join the horseman who set us free.

Quietly Comes the Blind Man Tapping

Quietly comes the blind man tapping

With his terrible red-tipped cane telling

Of his coming through light and darkness

As everyman stands silent in anxious

Anticipation of his terrible tapping

To where they are silently standing.

The Music and Colors of
Tom Crossley's World

Land of My Fathers
Welsh National Anthem

The land of my fathers, the land of my choice,
The land in which poets and minstrels rejoice;
The land where stern warriors were true to the core,
While bleeding for freedom of yore.

Wales! Wales! fav'rite land of Wales!
While sea her wall, may naught befall
To mar the old language of Wales.

Colliery Lad

Here before the Great War upon this very hill
A red winged dragon flag flaps
Above the gray stone Norman walls.
Against the sea blue sky
A sunstruck hawk shines copper
Circling Hovering Screaming Stooping
Into a field where a rabbit dodges
Between shocks of brown cornstalks
As far down the brilliant valley
A long drawn whinnying echoes
And echoes round the pale children
Leading little dappled ponies
Out of the coal black mines of Wales
Into the bright light and air
Whinnying.

Seaman

Out of the polar night they come
Round the savage sea curled Horn
Through lightning whirlwind and wave
Their five masted Windjammer rises and falls
Into the blue black wave walled valley's
Ceaseless roar and hiss and foam.
As high upon the royal mast
The oil skinned ice faced men sway
And glisten in the flashes of light.
Their blue hands cut red and dead to pain
Haul in the frozen square rigged sails
Holding hard to rope and yard.
But then the black returns with a whack
Of hail flaked knives cutting ripping
Away the shrieks of shredded sails
And of a man.

Farmer

Vermillioned autumn lights
Across the broad backs of two mules
Harnessed still as bronze
As a single red leaf floats slowly down
Onto the plowman's denimed lap
Beside his dog's flickering brown eyes.
Puffs of smoke rise from the plowman's pipe
Through his white mustache blinking his eyes
Watching the little ponies walking on waves of heat
Rising in strips of water over the brindled fields.
High above the plowman
The hawk screams again and again
As bursts of wind
Rustle the dry corn leaves like canvas
And the last rays of light ebb away

Into the distant whinnying
And the sharp bark of a dog
And a song sung in an ancient language.

Land of My Fathers

Old mountainous Cambria,the Eden of bards,
Each hill and each valley, excite my regards,
To the ears of her patriots how charming still seems
The music that flows in her streams.

My country tho' crushed by a hostile array,
The language of Cambria, lives out to this day.
The muse has eluded the traitors foul knives,
The harp of my country survives.

In The Meadow

There

In the meadow
I see a strong bowman

Standing alone

Shooting arrows
Of gold and silver

At the sun.

They miss
And fall back to earth

And all are lost.

As the sun sets

He searches
For them

Bending low
To the earth

In the meadow.

Leningrad 1941 – 42

Once
There were many children
Who were cold   so cold
At night
Their thin arms clung tight
Around mothers
Who were cold   so cold
While terrible dreams were dreamed
Of food
That was cold   so cold
So very cold
Many little sleds
Squeaked over snow
That was quiet   so quiet
And no laughter
Was laughed by riders
Who were quiet   so quiet
While sliding sliding toward
A place
That was quiet   so quiet
So very quiet
O children
Of Leningrad Beautiful Leningrad
Who are old   so old
So very old
May your children be warm with
Laughter

Around The Courthouse

Old men

Sitting

Spitting

Old men

Sunning

Funning

Old men

Sassing

Gassing

Old men

Joking

Smoking

Old men

Piddling

Whittling

Old men

Lying

Dying

In This My Eternal Crawl to Heaven

In this, my eternal crawl to heaven
I sing in praise of sin
And glory in its ding-dong bell
That rings for prodigal men,
Asleep on sow dipped hay beds,
As studded bed wet dreams
Jack their Jills on tumbling hills
Where shapes of thoughts are bled.

Then from this dry that's dripped its life,
They try their best to rise
With cross-cracked backs
Made human by Eden's crippling strife.
In this our eternal crawl to heaven
From which there is no end,
There's glory in the ding-dong bell
That rings for prodigal men.

Period Pieces

Flailing away
With flank and thigh
The mini legged
Mini beasts
Trip discreetly out
From under
Late Luther's
Cold black robes
To the heat
And the beat
Of the noon day fun
Where the sun
Never sets
On monks
With bad habits
And old dogs
Going mad
To walk on their hind legs
Behind
Behinds tripping
Ahead to where
They don't really care
As long as it leads
To period pieces
And glorious ends.

The Infidel That in Each Christian Lurks

The infidel that in each Christian lurks
Prays God his wisdom is not right.
The believer that in each sinner dwells
Fears at death His raging light.
Yet God and infidel alike
Owe homage to their dread,
For fear lies down with faith
And finds glory in their bed.

Crow Hunting

One last look from a dying crow's eye

reflects all within its spinning

fall from flock black and sky

blue through leaf green

and smoke white as

red red and red

flash fire

and fade

away

Sinkhole

Evening sun on feather sedge
Golden plumes round a sinkhole's edge

Broken china mixed with bones
Bits of white between gray stones

Old barbed fence of rusted wire
Wild roses and blackberry's wire

Surround this hole as a wall
But still a calf sometimes may fall

Into this deep sink to die
As black buzzards circle high

Year after year things are thrown
Into this hole as some unknown

Depth absorbs it all and so
Nothing stops the inward flow

Thank God the farmer needs his dump
For cans cars a useless pump

An old dried out bellyband
For a fine horse long gone and

A dead daughter's broken toy
A doll whose face lost its joy

Now this grave of dead machines
Darkens as the last sunbeams

Fade and little animals hide
From long smooth shadows that glide
Over these fields at eventide.

Cat's Cradle

Funny

how a straight piece of white string

with its ends

tied together

and woven

with the very best intentions

between eight fingers and two thumbs

on two hands

can end up

a bloody awful

mess.

Away Come Away

Away come away and together
let us sing the ancient way
of dreams filled with
unknown schemes
not conceived in books
but in joys and sorrows received
from listening to the winds
around and in us whirling.

Come, come with me I bid you come
and not be lonesome
but press your ear against the winds
that dispossess our dreams
from flesh and bone
until at last it seems
the whirling winds we have become
and know we are not dreaming.

My Lovely Lady's Eyes

My lovely Lady's eyes
Look in my eyes my eyes
My lovely Lady's eyes
See me see me in her eyes

My lovely Lady's eyes
Draw me into her eyes
Call me into her eyes
Call me into her eyes

Across the field her eyes
Call me call me into her eyes
Then she flies then she flies
Her wings and red tail flies

To my glove she flies
My Lady flies she flies
Looking into my eyes
Looking into my eyes

A Memory

A memory too much forever
On my hands and in my mind
Finds no hope in incredible longing
Yet pulls me down further into myself
Listening always for that sound
Sounding my name in whispers
And I cup my hands to catch that which is
Only memory and no more.

I see now and then quietly
That forever memory filtering its easy way
Through present things and future dreams
Until for a moment
I am there again completely
Not opposing not demanding
And as I turn to see more clearly
There is nothing but only memory.

Only One Son

Only one son

Now no more

Only one son

Off to war

Only one son

Heard the roar

Only one soldier

Now no more

Only one son

Now no more.

Head Druid's Annual Entrails Readings

On every twenty-first of June, all our folk
Gather together over at Big Oak,
For Head Druid's annual ox killing,
And Divine Order of Entrails Readings.

Entrails Readings used to be a super time,
Until Head Druid lost his mind;
There were ox ribs and mead, and sweet young girls,
And auguries augering better worlds.

But now, Head Druid is senile and has cataracts,
You can't trust his auguries always to be facts.
For example, I'll never believe him again when he sees,
Flights of eagles killed by bees.

Last year, he got us to believing we were those bees,
And get this, he convinced us those eagles were Roman armies.
Well that one got our arses whipped,
And I ended up hiding in a pit of shit.

Then there's those dumb-rocks he calls Stonehenge, that's where
He runs around in circles raving to the air,
"How does it go, how does it go…
Did I set it for Sun-ray…or was it Moon-glow?"

I don't let my children watch ox killings anymore,
There's too much violence, too much gore.
You're supposed to kill them with one whack,
But with Head Druid, it's HACK – HACK– HACK!

Since he got arthritis, he's lost his touch,
He drops the entrails entirely too much.
No wonder our future always looks scary,
The livers he reads are dirty and hairy.

Yesterday, when he announced he had crowned himself Head Fairy,
I decided that's enough, I'm moving over to Eire,
Where I hear St. Patrick is doing quite well,
And that it's a nice place to live, since he gave the snakes Hell!

The Great Revival of 1953

Dedicated to the 1953
Graduate Saints and Sinners
Of David Lipscomb High School

I do not remember much, nor remember very well,
But this I know for truth and this I'll truly tell,
Every year in high school chapel,
There was held a Great Revival.
A preacher came and preached of sin
And fire, that sinners burned forever in.
It scared the you know what out of me,
As I think it did you, for I still see
Us all hunkered deep down in our seats
Trying to hide, while the preacher entreats
Us to, "Turn from Satan's way!
Come, come now; be saved this very day!"
Then with his piercing eye, he held me long,
And sang, and sang, and sang, the invitation song:

> *"Almost persuaded, harvest is past!*
> *Almost persuaded, doom comes at last!*
> *Almost cannot avail; almost is but to fail,*
> *Sad, sad, that bitter wail – almost but lost!"*

O Lord, I almost died of fright,
If doom did not strike me then, I knew it would that night.
I prayed, "Feet rise up and walk! Dear Lord, do not let them fail.
I promise, I swear, I hear that bitter, *bitter wail.*
Feet, damn you, move - and preacher keep on singing.
I'll come forward, if my feet will get to springing."

Then it happened, there went one of you, then two, then three
    and four,
Then more, and more, and more.
A host of teenage sinners went rushing down the aisle.
All their feet were working, and their faces all did smile.
My time was running out, with fervor I did pray,
But still my feet of stone did stay, and stay, and stay.

"Sad, sad that bitter wail – almost but lost."

"*Lost…lost…lost*," echoed clearly, finally…and was gone.
Then silence, but for a whimper, that from my mouth was drawn.
I prayed, "Great God Almighty, don't let that song end there.
I promise I'm *persuaded*, but my feet won't work, I swear!"
His answer to my prayer came quickly, "Perchance,
Doth thou not remember all thy sneaking 'round to dance?"

The moral of this story is: Feet can lead you straight to hell.
So, since then, to warn others, I tell my terrible tale.
For what I've told you is the truth you see.
It happened to me, and it happened to thee, thou Class of '53.

These lines were composed while I was drunk
as a skunk, brought on by two six-packs of
Budweiser taken to check a run of bad luck.

"S.T."* Coldwater

The Rhyme of the Ancient Boozer

I drink and drink and drink a lot,
But never use crack and never smoke pot.
The only joints I ever use
Are on the county line where I abuse,

Budweiser regularly and sometimes Schlitz,
They're also where I have my fits.
Strange things I've seen and stranger heard,
But the worst of all is the Great Speckled Bird.

It giggles and sings a song that's quite jolly,
And then, Hot Damn, it turns into Miss Dolly.
She plays her guitar and shakes her gold hair,
Then she turns into the bird and giggles, "Beware!"

I rub my eyes but still it's there,
Flapping and circling me in the air,
Singing beer ads like the ones on TV.
Then without fail it shoots a bird at me.

Once, I pulled my gun and shot it twice,
Then for good measure I shot it thrice,
And it just giggled and giggled, "Penance more you'll do",
Then up around my neck it flew.

Now, I sit here a total wreck,
With this Great Speckled Bird around my neck,
It keeps goosing me with its tail,
And giggling, "It's fun to be with you in jail."

* "Severe Tremors" Coldwater

Red Robin Feathers

red

robin

feathers

on a

pond

make

me

wonder

where

she's

gone

A Dark Forest

Her life was spent finding faults in others.

She carried a large bag over her shoulder,

Filled with all of her injustices,

A load grown so heavy it bent her face forward,

Fixing her eyes upon the ground,

Searching the dirt for footprints

Of those who had done her wrong;

Their tracks were everywhere, making a wide trail

That led her far, far back into the fears of her life;

A path so deep she could not climb out,

Taking her deeper and deeper into the darkness,

As the bag grew heavier and heavier.

Song of Love

Between my thumbs
I hold a whistle
Of white hands
And green grass
Stretched tight
As all desire
And blow a sound
Of beauty and beauty
While birds
With all their songs
Curve down around
Like falling notes
And sing my song
Of love to you.

It's Thanksgiving 1969

It's Thanksgiving 1969

I'm sitting here
In our living room

Warm and well

Smoking my Oom Paul

Getting a little heady

Trying to write a poem
Worth reading
A hundred years from now

Or at least next week

Something moving
Pulls my attention
Outside to the woods

Through the twelve
Large windowpanes
I begin watching

Last summers leaves

Floating   falling
Brown and dry

They pile on top
Of others lying there
And start to disappear
It makes me a little sad
Knowing

But for the moment
I'm warm and well
And hear our children
Fussing and laughing

And your footsteps
In the bedroom above me.

Jackie

I want you to be here in the morning,
Warm and well and asleep,
In the bed beside me.

I want you to be here,
Just around the corner in the hall,
In your orange robe and gray slippers.

I want you to be here, so near
I can hear your beautiful voice say,
"Bubba's is my coffee ready?"

I want you to be here on the couch,
With Sally's head resting on your lap,
And see you hand reach out and pat her.

I want you to be here with me now,
Wiping the tears from my eyes,
So I can see you clearly.

I want you to be here beside me now,
Where I can feel you and hear you
Saying, over and over, again and again,
"Bubba's, my dear Bubba's, you're so precious."

My Last Breath

You help me

to my death

even as my last breath

leaves me

you are here lifting me

through the air

My Extinction

My extinction may come as surprise

Though it's happening before your eyes

For strange as it may be

I'm the very last one of me.

O Crown the Darkness Round

O crown the darkness round

With golden plumes of tears and joy

And nothing let us fear

For peaceful dreams join men

Across the empty space

With spinning stars

Til smiles of light surround

The angel's wings

And heads of beasts bow low

Before their King

Now born anew within the golden plumes